MANAGE YOUR EMOTIONS MASTER YOUR LIFE

A Therapist's Guide to Mental Well-Being, Happiness and Peace

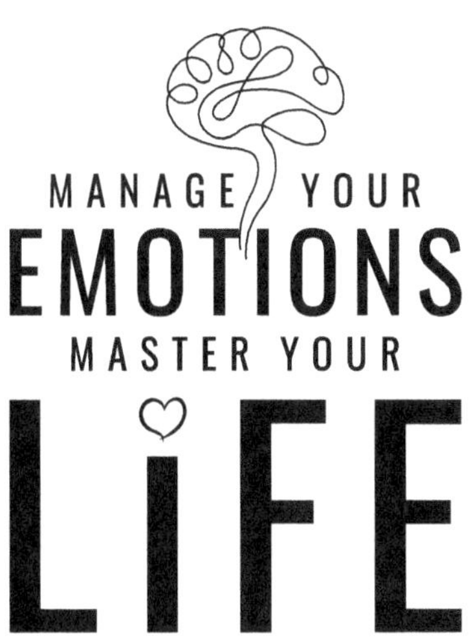

MANAGE YOUR EMOTIONS MASTER YOUR LiFE

A Therapist's Guide to Mental Well-Being,
Happiness and Peace

YASHI SONTHALIA

Worldwide Published by
Pendown Press

PENDOWN PRESS

An ISO 9001 & ISO 14001 Certified Co.,

Regd. Office: 2525/193, 1st Floor, Onkar Nagar-A,

Tri Nagar, Delhi-110035

Ph.: 09350849407, 09312235086

E-mail: info@pendownpress.com

Branch Office: 1A/2A, 20, Hari Sadan, Ansari Road,

Daryaganj, New Delhi-110002

Ph.: 011-45794768

Website: PendownPress.com

First Edition: 2023

ISBN: 978-93-5554-438-4

Layout and Cover Designed by Pendown Graphics Team

Printed and Bound in India by Thomson Press India Ltd.

Dedicated to each one of you readers who chose this book and in turn chose happiness and peace.

Your courage and patience inspires me.

Contents

Chapter 4

Chapter 5

Author's Note

Hi!

While you can get to know me better in the Preface & "About the Author" section of the book, I just wanted to take a minute to sincerely thank you for picking this book up and giving it a chance. As you give this book a chance, you are also giving one to yourself, which means a lot.

There may be several emotions you may feel as you find your way through this journey, as did I, and I hope you will be open to experiencing them and listening to what they have to say.

I am proud of you for all that you've done for yourself and those around you. I see you, I hear you, and I appreciate you.

I hope that by the end of this book, if you take only one thing away, then that is to remember that no matter where you are or what you may be feeling and experiencing, you are not alone. Not only is there someone who understands and relates, but also someone who empathizes and someone who is willing to reach out and help you.

Feel free to connect with me on Instagram or my email ID, mentioned at the end, along with other details about me. I'd love to hear from you about your experience with this book.

Thank you,

Empathetically Yours

Yashi Sonthalia

How It All Came About

Hi, I am Yashi, and I am a therapist.

Often I am asked this question as to what made me choose this particular profession. **To begin with, let me share that this is not merely a profession for me; it is the passion of purpose that drives me.**

I chanced upon the field of psychology when I was in school. It was almost as if the universe was nudging me in the right direction. I was at that stage of life where I knew what I did not want my life to look like but did not have complete clarity on what it should look like.

Going through the routine turbulence of teenage, the need for understanding and empathy was critical, and the field of mental health appeared to me to be a milestone in the direction of what I wanted my life to look like. I felt it would be fulfilling to be able to extend to others the support and empowerment that I myself craved.

As I started my studies in psychology, it opened up a whole new and wondrous universe to me. I found myself questioning many things. I realized how some of our learnings and ways of living could be so stunting and invalidating for our mental health. In fact, it was surprising how casually we sometimes end up shaming and invalidating others and ourselves, even without knowing that we are doing so.

Psychology came knocking on my door at an opportune time, right when I was on the threshold of making career decisions. As I neared my graduation, I began to view life from a very different perspective. And so I began my journey as a therapist as a quest with too many questions and not many answers.

This questioning and seeking attitude led me to study deeper and have conversations with as many people as I could. Having conversations with so many people from such different walks of life made me realize how similar we all are in our very essence of being. All we want is to be seen and heard. All we need is a little care and compassion.

I remember talking to a client who said, "I am not good enough. And every interaction lately has become a reminder of that. I don't know if I am even worthy of what I am doing right now in my career or in my personal life." That was a pivotal moment for me. I walked out of that session, struggling to make sense of how our view of our own worth and self can become so lopsided.

"I don't know how to reply to that, Yashi, I don't know how I am feeling. Isn't it good that I am not an emotional fool?" This was the reply another client gave me with a humorless laugh when we were trying to explore the kind of emotions a particularly difficult incident elicited in him. "Is that right?" I remember wondering to myself as I ended the session. Why is vulnerability seen as such a weakness, and why is indulging and acknowledging our emotions such a taboo?

These are just glimpses of the 400+ hours of such conversations I have had so far.

Such conversations and interactions have only strengthened my resolve to continue working dedicatedly in the field of mental health.

So, here comes scenario 2:

Take a look at my conversations with the same clients sometime later-

"I was able to celebrate my day for me, and that's a first in 10 years, Yashi! You know, I think I alone decide my worth. I know who I am, and that seems to be enough for now." This was how my last conversation with that first client went a week ago.

Want a glimpse of how the second client is doing right now?

"I am allowed to feel. And I have started to feel so alive ever since I internalized that Yashi. It's difficult on some days, but it's so much better than the numbness."

And the best part about being a therapist is that I get to grow and imbibe new learnings along with my clients. You see, without a doubt, there is so much for me to take away from these sessions, both as a therapist and as an individual.

Back then, after these initial conversations, here's what I found for myself to take away, reflect on and learn from: I realized a sense of emotional deprivation and lack of prioritizing our own self seemed to have become the norm. Constantly governed by shoulds and musts, I, too, wasn't in touch with my emotions and had a skewed self-image.

If I take a moment to reflect now, I think I owe my growth ever since that moment to every single individual I met in my practice.

Building on the empathy, the endless support and the encouragement I had received from my parents and then my training as a therapist helped me give myself the space to reconsider the questions I had begun my journey with.

Many of those questions, I realized, were answers in themselves. My sense of self shifted, and I had a whole new perspective to work with.

I have realized I am a work in progress. I am allowed to take my time, to grow, to change and to just be. I have a long way to go for me, and I am looking forward to it.

A few months back, when my father suggested I write a book since I always have so much to share with everyone I meet, it got me thinking. **I realized if there was one thing I wish people knew, it was this:**

The value of emotions and their own worth.

And that's all I wish to say here. The rest is contained in the five open letters nestled between the pages of this book for you to go through, absorb, reflect on and apply at your own time and pace.

This book is an attempt to share this journey of mine with you in a way that it leaves you with a few answers and a whole lot of self-compassion.

Before You Start

Hi!

What you are about to dive into are 5 letters that I have written for you as a therapist, a friend and primarily as someone who has felt what you are feeling and relates to you.

Following the letters and spread in between are 10+ activities and exercises for you to try at your own pace to add to your experience of reading these letters and for you to have a bigger takeaway from this journey. I hope these letters deliver to you the empathy, understanding, compassion and respect I have for you.

As you get started, I encourage you to gather all your supplies: highlighters, pens, colors, sticky notes and whatever else you may need to make this journey unique, personal and impactful for you. The last two pages have been intentionally left blank for just this purpose.

Most importantly, I hope you begin this experience with an open mind and as much compassion and love as you can gather for yourself.

Lastly, thank you for giving me this opportunity to share this tiny bit of myself with you and for letting it feel understood.

About the Author

Yashi Sonthalia is a counseling psychologist. She has completed her Master's in Psychology with a specialization in Counseling.

She also holds a Diploma in Positive Psychology and has completed several certificate courses in various other areas in the field of mental health.

She currently works as a therapist and also works with content and conducts webinars.

She is an avid reader, loves the world of fiction and enjoys her share of music and k-dramas. She also loves spending time with her family and friends.

She strongly believes in normalizing mental health and having conversations about it. One of her main principles revolves around the idea of self-compassion and building a healthy relationship with oneself.

yashi_sonthalia

reachouttoyashi@gmail.com

Acknowledgement

To begin with, I would like to thank my parents and my family for being my biggest inspiration and my pillars of strength throughout. I owe who I am to them.

I would also like to extend my gratitude to my mentors and my clients who have always shown faith in me and given me the space to grow and learn.

Lastly, I would like to acknowledge myself, for believing in me and for taking this leap of faith.

1.1 When You Feel Angry

What you are feeling is allowed. It is okay to feel this way. I can imagine how this feeling of anger seems to be eating you up on the inside, wanting to burst out in its entirety.

I hear how you want to protect yourself, stand up for yourself and against all that hurt you, and is piercing you even at this moment. You may be trembling with the force of your anger, practicing physical restraint to hold it in. Maybe you have already let some of it out; maybe this is round two. I hear you.

We, as a society have villainized anger. We glorify its absence and condemn its presence. And in an effort to then fit in, to be considered "normal", we push the anger away. We turn our back on this emotion.

However, the lack of acknowledgement does not result in it going away. Often, this emotion stays where it is, unheard and unattended to. And as this cycle of blissful (or effortful) ignorance continues, the anger piles up.

It stays where it is, unheard and unattended to. And this often becomes the calm before the storm. What may follow, but is not limited to, is an outburst where you lash out with an intensity you could never have imagined. You react in a manner that is considered inappropriate or unwarranted. What may also follow is the anger taking a form that you don't recognize. It comes out as harsh criticism, passive aggression, or even self-harm.

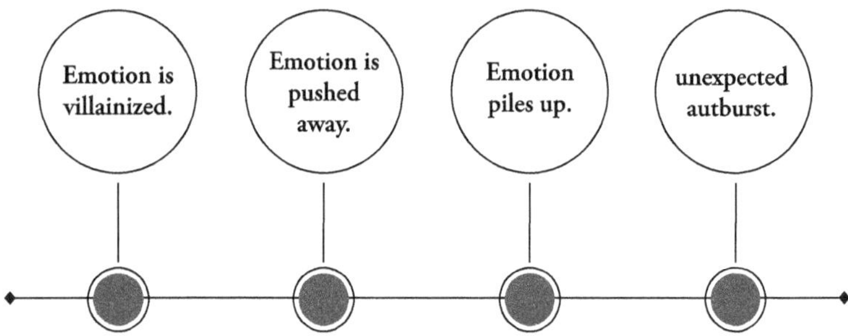

Anger is an emotion like any other. It is a feeling, and just like any other feeling, it comes, washes over you and leaves. It passes. That's how feelings work. However, when we become ignorant of this feeling of anger and block it away, it stays. It does not get a chance to come out, to be expressed, and so it builds. Each wave builds up as it is restrained. But then, what do you do with this emotion?

Use this space below to describe how you feel when angry. You can use colors, words, analogies, drawings, or whatever helps you express it in its authenticity.

As I mentioned earlier, anger is just an emotion. It holds as much functional value as any other emotion would. And in that sense, feeling angry is okay. It is a very normal emotion to experience and to allow yourself to feel. You can begin with just this reminder: It's okay for me to feel this way. It is also very important to then express what you are feeling, to be able to let it out, to let it wash over you and leave. There are several healthy and adaptive ways of expressing and working through this feeling of anger.

I am going to list a few here. You can always work with your therapist to identify which method may be best suited for you based on your situation.

- Communicate it using "I" statements

- Put the feelings down on a piece of paper. You can write, draw, scribble or tear.

- Talk to someone, and find a safe space to let what you are feeling out. Focus on the present moment, either using your breath, a mantra, a thought or even a thing as an anchor.

- Allow yourself to cry it out.

 # 1.2 *Exercises*

1.2.1 *Identifying Your Anger Buttons*

I want you to take some time to observe what pushes your anger buttons. This simply means you take some time to notice what triggers an anger response in you. This will not only help you narrow down the situations but also help you identify the source of the emotion, thus letting you work on it better.

1.2.2 Dealing With Anger 101

Now that you've taken your time to explore what triggers the anger emotion within you let's take some time to explore both prevention and cure. What we intend to do here is to see if we can prevent this anger response by shifting something in the environment or the trigger itself as well as identifying what can be done to allow ourselves to work through this emotion when it arises so that it is processed and finds it's way out of your system.

Here's an example; for the anger button mentioned earlier, this is how the emotion can be expressed productively:

- *Communicate with my team members about the recently missed deadline using "I" statements using a solution-focused approach.*

2.1 When You Feel Like Unbottling

We often prioritize our relationships with everyone around us and spend much of our time exploring what in our environment contributes to how we feel about many things, including ourselves, so much so that we are lost in that endless maze before taking the time to build a relationship with ourselves.

Take a minute to reflect and circle the number which appropriately describes your relationship with yourself on a scale of 0-10, with 0 being the most negative to 10 being the best relationship possible.

You end up spending so much time wanting to make sure that people view you in a certain way and hold a certain perspective about you that you often forget to check in with yourself to establish how you see yourself first. It is almost as if your perception of yourself is only a culmination of how you think those around you see you and nothing as a constant sense of self you took your time to understand and identify.

The idea of taking some time to sit with yourself and your thoughts overwhelms you, the idea of taking some time to get in touch with your emotions scares you and the idea of knowing yourself in the way that only you can as you know your story disturbs you. You have taken so much time and effort to avoid this storm that has been brewing on the inside.

You are afraid to allow yourself to sit, to pause, to embrace or to allow what comes your way. You find it so difficult to even acknowledge your own effort in bringing that joy to your life, for that would mean you see it, you take responsibility for it and what would happen if you lose it then?

Let's take a minute here to reflect and recall certain questions, situations or even emotions that make us feel uncomfortable or those we tend to avoid.

I hear you. These thoughts and emotions can be so internalized that on a good day, they are beneath so many layers you wouldn't know of their existence. And yet, on the days they become apparent, you are left feeling so small, unheard, or misunderstood.

How about you just take a minute right now to pause? Take that breath in and let it out. When you distance yourself so much from your own emotions, you end up tuning out. How about we take a minute to tune in? How about you take a minute to ask yourself this question: how are you feeling right now? How have you been doing lately?

And before you jump to the automated response, genuinely be open to hearing what you have to say. How does it feel to just hear your genuine answer, no matter how ugly or beautiful it is?

Can you give yourself this one opportunity to have this safe space with yourself that you are so easily able to create for others to just be honest, to just be vulnerable, to just be authentic, to just be? It's okay to do all of this. No matter how difficult or wrong it may feel, you are actually allowed to just be, to take that break before you are off to catch up in whatever race you have set yourself up to.

How about you try to hold yourself in the eyes of your mind and hear yourself out? Can you give yourself the liberty to cry it out and to let it be? It's okay to feel. The intensity of your own emotions may take you aback. But through it all, you could choose to repeat to yourself: I am allowed to feel it is okay. I am here.

How are you feeling right now?

How have you been doing lately?

I am allowed to feel, it is okay. I am here.

2.2 Exercises

2.2.1 Feeling Statements

Allowing yourself to accept your feelings and acknowledging them can go a long way toward processing them and moving ahead. Therefore, I encourage you to use the rest of this space to write down for yourself statements that you would expect someone to say to you or what you say to others when you/they are feeling a certain way, especially when it is an emotion you/they face difficulty working with. You can then constantly bring yourself back to these statements as a way to open the bottle and let yourself feel.

Here's an example:

- *This has been tiring, and I am feeling drained.*

2.2.2 Affirming Your Experiences

Affirmations are a very simple, straightforward yet effective method to work on your perceptions. Affirmations are an attempt to rewire your mind, and create a muscle memory that focuses on creating the right mindset for you to fall back to. Listed below are a few examples of affirmations you can use in the context of allowing yourself to feel and experience:

- *My emotions are valid.*
- *I am allowed to acknowledge my feelings.*
- *My experiences are authentic.*

You can use the statements above as they are or use them as a guideline to build your own affirmations, which you can then use on a regular basis.

3.1 When You Feel Invalidated

Do you have conversations that leave you feeling frustrated? It usually begins with us sharing our thoughts, opinions and feelings, but somewhere along the way, things get a little heated. Opinions are pushed, and belittling statements are exchanged. Towards the end, we start to feel misunderstood, overwhelmed or unheard.

The entire experience leaves us feeling invalidated or even lost. This often happens in situations where we are expressing ourselves candidly to others, especially to those we consider close. Feeling misunderstood may lead us to distance ourselves from the other person, start to question our own opinions and emotions or even make us feel very isolated and upset.

Unlike me, he thinks it's okay. Probably I am not getting this right.

Are you serious? What you said does not even make sense.

Aren't you exaggerating it a little? It's not even that big of a deal.

I am the only one with this opinion. I don't think I made the right decision.

I probably shouldn't be feeling that way. She finds it wrong.

I hear you. It makes you feel like you'd rather not communicate at all than go through this. You start to hold back on your own thoughts or opinions. In some situations, it even results in you wanting to make others see things your way. It feels only right for them to see how you also make sense and push them in that direction.

Let me ask you my favorite question. If we were to meet in a restaurant and I was feeling cold while you were feeling hot, would you tell me I am wrong to be feeling cold? Would you stop me from putting on my jacket? Your answer is probably no. Why? Because we are experiencing the same temperature differently, and that is okay. The fact of the temperature being a certain degree does not change, yet how the both of us experience it can look immensely different. This makes neither of us wrong or right. It just makes us two individuals who experience things differently.

You may be curious about why I am feeling cold and ask me about the same. However, you probably wouldn't try to convince me to start feeling hot or be upset with me about this fact. You also wouldn't question why you were feeling hot and if that makes sense anymore.

Let's take a minute to note a few incidents where you have observed this happening with you. What has been "cold" for you but "hot" for someone else?

Hot   Cold

The similar is true for many of our conversations and situations. Many a time, our opinions, thoughts, experiences or emotions about a certain something do not align with the people we meet. And that's okay. It does not have to. You are allowed to experience life in your unique way and build your version of reality from it. It is the way we all function. And that's your second reminder. We all function similarly only in the sense that our realities look different and unique to each of us based on the versions we build through our experiences. Therefore, we are allowed to agree to disagree and respect each other's and our own realities.

What we can do in such situations is show genuine curiosity to explore how the other has built their reality. We can continue to hold our own reality while we respect others for theirs. However, in situations where how one sees something has a direct effect on you or vice versa, you are allowed to put your point across and invite the other to put theirs and then explore a middle ground which is okay with the both of you. This may mean a little accommodation of their reality into yours, just like it would be for them. The point is to make sure you feel accommodated and also make the other feel the same in such situations.

4.1 Read When You Feel Unproductive

Feeling overwhelmed has become the new normal lately. With the current hustle culture that we are living in, where productivity and results have become the bottom line, we are often left feeling tired on the good days and inadequate and drained out on the bad ones. The need to constantly be doing something and have the results speak for us has made it very difficult to prioritize ourselves or the journey in any manner.

Along with this comes the way productivity is defined in a very narrow sense. Put together; we are often left feeling the constant need to do more, to be more without being able to take any moment to pause and reflect on our journeys, take any break or even evaluate the utility of the productivity we often end up chasing.

The most difficult aspect of it all is dealing with the fatigue and dissatisfaction that becomes a constant part of our lives. You start to feel so tired and thoroughly exhausted at any given time, which then interferes with your effectiveness and hence, adds to the discontentment you are already feeling since it never is enough, and you end up finding yourself stuck in a vicious cycle. We become trapped in this cycle of wanting more and never finding anything enough.

Even the idea of taking a break or pausing for a minute sounds preposterous. The critic within you jumps at the idea, asking you what have you even accomplished to be wanting a break or considering what you have done to be enough. The chase never ends.

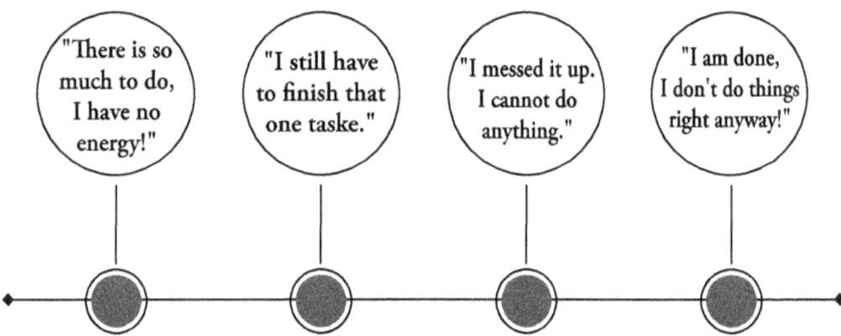

I hear you. It is so exhausting that there are days when you just want to give up. You want to stop, leave it all and just lie down. You want to have a minute of peace and calm in this constant chaos of more and more. It becomes difficult to keep going. And underlying all these thoughts is still the feeling of it not being enough, you not being enough.

We, as humans, work in numbers. It is easier to do the tougher thing as a group than to do the easier thing as an individual. Hence, we jump into this endless race of productivity with everyone else. However, while it is awkward to be the only one doing things differently, why not add a little more awareness to this mindless race?

Why not introduce the idea of taking care of yourself to the definition of productivity? Productivity can mean all that it already does and more. It can include self-care, taking breaks for self, moments of pause and so on. Why not choose productive goals with a little more awareness?

Your goals can be more in line with your ultimate destination, they can be more practical, and they can definitely be more flexible and still continue to be productive goals. Why not acknowledge the goals you have accomplished? You can take your time to look back and reflect on your journey so far and appreciate yourself for it.

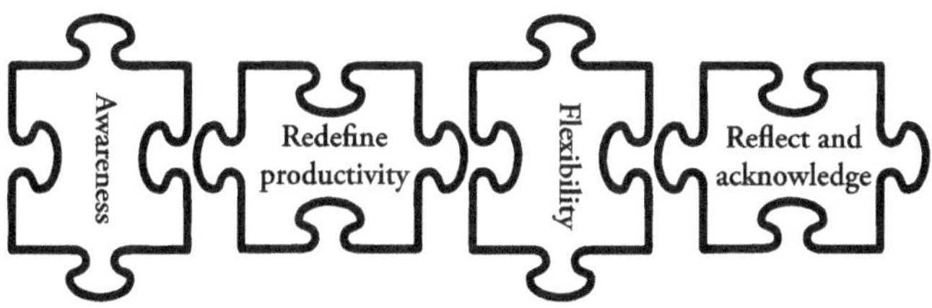

While it may be a little too much to ask yourself to break away from this way of living completely, you are allowed to make it easier and more fulfilling for yourself. You are allowed.

 # 4.2 Exercises

4.2.1 Acknowledgment Letter to Self

When you acknowledge yourself and your efforts, it makes the entire process that much more fulfilling and motivating. So, how about you use the rest of this space to write yourself an acknowledgement letter? You can also definitely make this a regular practice in your life.

4.2.2 River of Life

I want you to use the rest of this page to create a river that symbolizes your life. It can begin with your birth or any significant moment of your life. You can use trees, boulders, rocks, tributaries, etc., to mark the significant events, people and other such aspects of your life. Take a moment to reflect on the river you see at the end of this process.

Chapter 5

5.1 Read When You Feel Unworthy

How do you see yourself? If you were to take a minute to score the worth you attach to yourself on a scale of 0-10, what would it be?

⓪ ① ② ③ ④ ⑤ ⑥ ⑦ ⑧ ⑨ ⑩

Do you often feel like you are not good enough? Do you find it difficult to take someone's praise at face value and end up assuming an ulterior motive from their end? Do you find it difficult to get started on any task since you've assumed that you wouldn't be able to do it well anyway? Do you always assume that the others are right since they would obviously know better than you? The way you see your own worth and your self-esteem plays a very important role in multiple areas of your life.

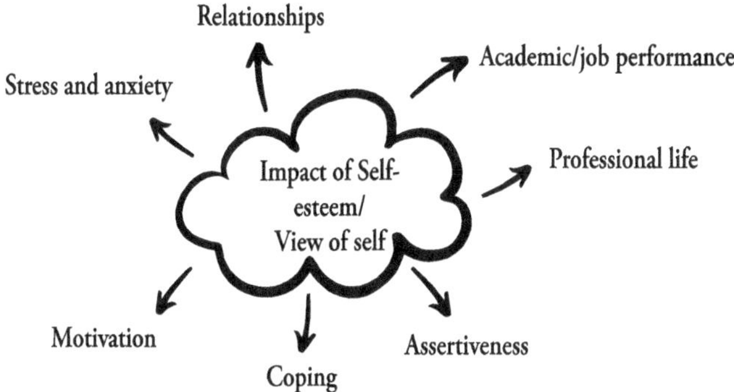

When you are not sure of yourself and not confident in your own worth and capabilities, it makes it very arduous to find the motivation to do anything, to be with yourself and even to spend time around others. You end up wanting to escape every situation when what you are really trying to escape is this constant feeling of not being good enough or worthy in any situation or context.

Therefore, the bottom line is finding that space of comfort and pride in being yourself, in being in your own skin. It means you start to acknowledge what you are deserving of and what you are worthy of. When you start to give yourself the kind of respect, esteem and space you deserve, it becomes much easier for others to follow suit.

Let's just take a minute to turn the tables around. Take a minute to think of all the people you love. Think of all that they are as an individual and everything you love about them. There is a possibility that you also recall their shortcomings or things about them that upset you. Now, ask yourself if that makes you respect or love them any less. When you hold others with a certain sense of respect and compassion irrespective of who they are, why not hold yourself with the same kind of regard?

Why end up making the effort of holding two different standards, two different points of view, one for yourself and one for others? You are allowed to treat yourself with the same kind of regard and respect you treat those around you with.

Here's an example of how you would possibly react to your friend not scoring their aimed score on a test:

Hey, I messed up, I couldn't even get a decent score.

Hey, you did your best. You even cracked it. I am proud of you.

However, if the same were to happen to you, your thoughts may sound something like this:

We are a culmination of all of our experiences, perceptions, beliefs, values and learnings. Going back to my favorite example, if we were to meet at a restaurant and perceive the temperature differently, it wouldn't make either of us wrong or any less. Our perceptions are bound to differ. We are different people. And it is this difference, this uniqueness, that makes you that bit more special. You are allowed to hold this uniqueness close to who you are. You are worthy of your own acknowledgement, gratitude, praise and appreciation.

We often take all that we do as being nothing or not enough. It is very easily taken for granted. Let's take an example when a waiter at a restaurant brings you your food, I am sure you say thank you. The same also occurs when you are paying for a bill or when you get a door delivery for something. Why do we thank these individuals? It is a matter of courtesy, yes. You also observe that they are helping you out in some manner, they are doing what they are meant to be doing, and we appreciate that. And that's it.

When we can express gratitude to another individual for doing something for us that was meant to be done, why not also do that for ourselves? You can thank yourself for waking up, for braving through a tough day, for meeting a particularly stressful deadline; you can thank yourself. You are allowed to treat yourself with the same kind of respect, love, care and compassion that you treat those around you with.

5.2 Exercises

5.2.1 Circle of Emotions

Here are two circles. I want you to fill both of them with moments or events you can recall that made you feel the emotion as mentioned in the circles. As you do this exercise, I encourage you to also close your eyes and go back to each of those moments and stay there for a minute, letting yourself feel those emotions again. You can always find your way back to these circles to walk down memory lane and relive those emotions.

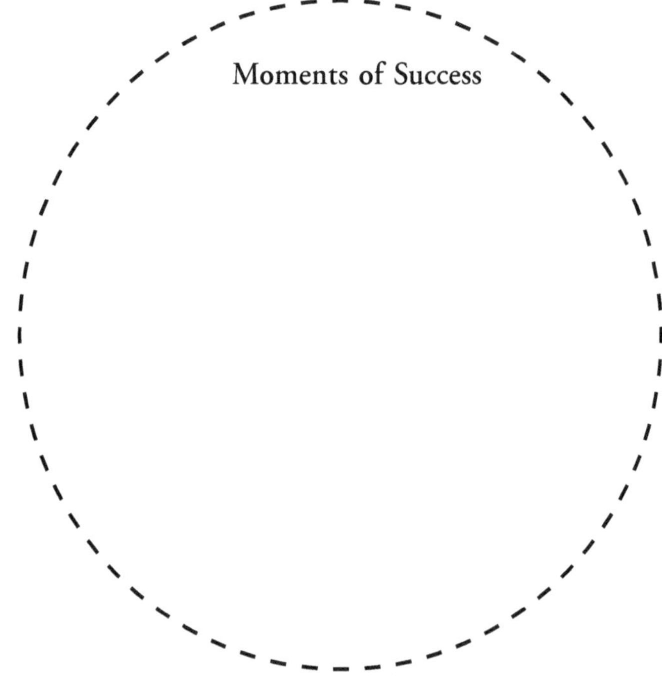

Moments of Peace

5.2.2 Esteem Journal Prompts

I want you to try answering one of these prompts every day. You can select one for each day and can also repeat the same one multiple times.

- *Something I did well today:*
- *I feel proud when:*
- *Today, I accomplished:*
- *Something I did for someone:*
- *I feel good about myself when:*
- *Today was interesting because:*
- *A positive thing I witnessed:*
- *Something someone did for me:*

Congratulations

Hooray!

You've successfully made your way to the end of this experience. Let's take a minute to let that sink in.

I hope this journey was as insightful and eye-opening for you as it was for me. And I know I said that you've come to an end, but I would love for you to try this one last exercise as you put this book away (for now, for you can always find your way back to it. We all need those doses of reminders after all).

I encourage you to use the rest of this space to write yourself a letter about how this experience was for you. You could talk about the emotions you felt, your key takeaways, a thank you here, a woohoo there, whatever comes to you.